"Thanks" is one of the happiest
and most heartfelt words
anyone can say. It may be
just one little word, but within
those six letters are so many
smiles, sweet feelings, and very
wonderful thoughts.

— J. Kalispell

Blue Mountain Arts®

New and Best-Selling Titles

By Susan Polis Schutz:
To My Daughter with Love on the Important Things in Life
To My Son with Love

By Douglas Pagels:
For You, My Soul Mate
Required Reading for All Teenagers
The Next Chapter of Your Life
You Are One Amazing Lady

By Marci:
Angels Are Everywhere!
Friends Are Forever
10 Simple Things to Remember
To My Daughter
To My Granddaughter
To My Mother
To My Sister
You Are My "Once in a Lifetime"

By Wally Amos, with Stu Glauberman:
The Path to Success Is Paved with Positive Thinking

By Minx Boren:
Healing Is a Journey

By M. Butler and D. Mastromarino:
Take Time for You

By Carol Wiseman:
Emerging from the Heartache of Loss

Anthologies:
A Daughter Is Life's Greatest Gift
A Son Is Life's Greatest Gift
Dream Big, Stay Positive, and Believe in Yourself
God Is Always Watching Over You
God Loves You Just the Way You Are
Hang In There
The Love Between a Mother and Daughter Is Forever
Nothing Fills the Heart with Joy like a Grandson
There Is Nothing Sweeter in Life Than a Granddaughter
Think Positive Thoughts Every Day
When I Say I Love You
Words Every Woman Should Remember

A Daybook of

Gratitude

How to Live Each Day
with a Thankful Heart

A Blue Mountain Arts® Collection

Edited by Becky McKay

Blue Mountain Press™

Boulder, Colorado

Library of Congress Control Number: 2014942669
ISBN: 978-1-59842-840-7

◫ and Blue Mountain Press are registered in U.S. Patent and Trademark Office.
Certain trademarks are used under license.

Printed in China.
Second Printing: 2015

Blue Mountain Arts, Inc.

P.O. Box 4549, Boulder, Colorado 80306

Contents

Live Every Day with a Thankful Heart

Greet each day with a grateful heart. Imagine your future. Make some new plans. Remember your uniqueness. Reflect on how much you are loved.

Do something fun, special, magical, and memorable. Pretend it's your very own holiday. Appreciate your gifts. Recognize your talents. Concentrate on you today. Be thankful for what makes you <u>you</u>.

The greatest gift you've been given is you. Celebrate yourself... with hope, with joy, with appreciation. Dare to dream. Open your heart and let yourself go as far as your mind will take you. Drop any regrets and negative thoughts that hold you down.

Count your blessings; love your life; treasure your family and friends and all that you're thankful for. Above all, soak in the present of each moment and give thanks with all your heart.

— Donna Fargo

Ten Ways to Cultivate Gratitude

1. Realize that life isn't always fair. Accept what you must, and change what you can.

2. Think before you act. A moment of carelessness or anger can cause years of anguish and regret.

3. Look for the beauty in life, in people, in nature, and in yourself.

4. Appreciate what you have: the people, the opportunities, the material possessions.

5. Make the effort to have fun. It's a great way to bond with others, and it makes some of the best memories.

6. Set aside some time for yourself. Do something you enjoy without feeling even a little guilty.

7. Accept others without judgment. Everyone is unique, and it's okay to be different.

8. Forgive. Bitterness and resentment hurt you more than the person you direct them at.

9. Learn. Open your mind to new ideas and activities, and don't be afraid to try.

10. Dream. Make plans, believe in yourself, and go for what you want.

— Barbara Cage

What Does "Thank You" Really Mean?

"Thank you" is one of those wonderful phrases
people use to express a special gratitude.
But there's often a lot more to it
than those two words can say.

When it comes from the heart,
from deep inside
the nicest feelings
and the most special thoughts,
"thank you" means so much.

It means thank you for taking the time
to show that you care.
It means "you really made my day,"
and sometimes it means that you
really make all the days
so much better.
It means you make me feel so nice,
and I wish I could
do the same for you...
just by letting you know how much
you mean to me.

"Thank you" means you didn't have to...
but I'm so grateful that you did.
"Thank you" means that you've done
something special that
I'll never forget.

— Chris Gallatin

Welcome Each Blessing

Be thankful when your blessings
   far outnumber your reasons to cry;
when sorrow leaves and healing begins;
when those clouds overhead pass on by
and leave only sunshine in your life.

Be thankful when you think that you can't go on
but find the strength inside;
when that flicker of hope appears
   to push away your doubts;
when everything has been deemed lost,
but you discover that what matters most
can never be taken from you —
because it rests inside your heart
warmly, safely, and secured with love.

Be thankful when someone you love
loves you in return;
when that one certain smile is turned your way;
and when you are singled out as someone
 who is unique, cared for, and appreciated.

Be thankful for the blessings in your life
and count them often.
For when you welcome each one
with a grateful heart,
you'll find them continuing
to flow into your life every day.

— Barbara J. Hall

How to Write "Thank You" In...

French:	Merci
Spanish:	Gracias
Italian:	Grazie
Japanese:	ありがとうございます。
German:	Danke schön
Russian:	Спасибо
Dutch:	Dank u
Mandarin Chinese:	谢 谢
Swedish:	Tack
Arabic:	شكرا
Hebrew:	תודה
Norwegian:	Tusen takk
Polish:	Dziękuję
Greek:	Ευχαριστω

"Thanks" is one of the happiest and most heartfelt words anyone can say. It may be just one little word, but within those six letters are so many smiles, sweet feelings, and very wonderful thoughts.

— J. Kalispell

There Are
So Many Things to
Be Thankful For...

- ๑ Family

- ๑ Great friends

- ๑ Meaningful work

- ๑ Good health

- ๑ Love

- ๑ Intimacy

- ๑ Blue skies

- Waterfalls

- Kindness

- Summer storms

- Compassion

- Autumn leaves

- Flowers in bloom

- Full moons

- Happiness

We don't often
take the time out of our busy lives
to think about all
the beautiful things
and to be thankful for them
If we did reflect on these things
we would realize how very
lucky and fortunate we really are

I am very thankful
for the love of my husband —
which is so complete and fulfilling
and is based on honesty, equality
intellectualism and romance

I am very thankful
for the love of my children —
which is all encompassing
and is based on teaching, tenderness
sensitivity, caring and hugging

I am very thankful
that I am able to love
and that the love is returned to me

I am very thankful
that I am healthy
and that the people I love
are healthy

I am very thankful
that I have dreams to follow
and goals to strive for...

I am very thankful
for the beauty of nature —
magnificent mountains
the colorful leaves
the smell of flowers
the roaring of the waves
the setting sun
the rising moon

Everywhere I look
I see the wonders of nature
and I feel so proud
to be a small part of it

I am very thankful
for all the good people in the world
I am very thankful
that I have good friends

I am very thankful
to be alive
in a time when
we can make the world
a better place
to live in
— Susan Polis Schutz

There Is Good
to Be Found
in All Situations

There is good in life every day.
Take a few minutes to distract yourself
from your concerns —
long enough to draw strength from a tree
or to find pleasure in a bird's song.

Return a smile;
realize that life is a series of levels,
cycles of ups and downs —
some easy, some challenging.
Through it all, you will learn;
you will grow strong in faith;
you will mature in understanding.
The difficult times are often
the best teachers, and there is
good to be found in all situations.

— Pamela Owens Renfro

Focus on the Favorable

The secret of gratitude is unbelievably simple: when we focus on the favorable, there is less room for the regrettable. By maximizing our blessings instead of our desires, we discover that life's small gifts really can impact our happiness.

A life of gratitude starts with a single grateful thought. And then another. And another...

— Elizabeth Rose

Let us rise up and be thankful,
for if we didn't learn a lot today,
at least we learned a little,
and if we didn't learn a little,
at least we didn't get sick,
and if we got sick,
at least we didn't die;
so, let us be thankful.
— Buddha

Don't Take Anything for Granted

Today, smile at your life and your choices. Don't worry about the paths you should have taken or the opportunities you ignored. Instead, breathe in the life that surrounds you — let it fill your soul with light and hope.

Life can be so busy, and we sometimes take for granted the important little things that make us smile. Look at the sunset, share a cup of coffee with your best friend, or hear the wind rustle through the trees. Take some time to listen to life and feel the sun on your face. Stop to watch butterflies in your garden.

The gifts of beauty, inspiration, love, and reflection are all around you.

— Carol Schelling

Choose an Attitude of Gratitude

Your living is determined not so much by what life brings to you as by the attitude you bring to life; not so much by what happens to you as by the way your mind looks at what happens.

Circumstances and situations do color life, but you have been given the mind to choose what the color will be.

— John Homer Miller

He is a wise man who does not grieve for
the things which he has not, but rejoices for
those which he has.

— Epictetus

Some people are always grumbling because
roses have thorns. I am thankful that thorns
have roses.

— Alphonse Karr

One Day at a Time

Our lives are made up of a million moments, spent in a million different ways. Some are spent searching for love, peace, and harmony. Others are spent surviving day to day. But there is no greater moment than when we find that life — with all its joys and sorrows — is meant to be lived one day at a time.

It's in this knowledge that we discover the most wonderful truth of all. Whether we live in a forty-room mansion, surrounded by servants and wealth, or find it a struggle to manage the rent month to month, we have it within our power to be fully satisfied and live a life with true meaning.

One day at a time — we have that ability through cherishing each moment and rejoicing in each dream. We can experience each day anew, and with this fresh start, we have what it takes to make all of our dreams come true. Each day is new, and living one day at a time enables us to truly enjoy life and live it to the fullest.

— Regina Hill

Let Go of How You Think Life Should Be

We are haunted by an ideal life, and it is because we have within us the beginning and the possibility of it.

— Phillips Brooks

Don't focus on what was.
Look forward to what can be,
and then do all you can to make it a reality.
Life is what you make of it,
and the challenges that come your way
are just opportunities to right what is wrong.
Don't get discouraged, and don't give up.
You have it all inside yourself,
and you can overcome anything
if you put your mind to it.

— Paula Michele Adams

Be Content with What You Have

There are nine requisites
   for contented living:
Health enough to make
   work a pleasure.
Wealth enough
   to support your needs.
Strength enough to battle with
   difficulties and overcome them.
Grace enough to confess
   your sins and forsake them.

Patience enough to toil
    until some good is accomplished.
Charity enough to see
    some good in your neighbor.
Love enough to move you
    to be useful and helpful to others.
Faith enough to make real
    the things of God.
Hope enough to remove all
    anxious fears concerning the future.

— Johann Wolfgang von Goethe

You're Richer Than You Think...

If you spend most of your waking hours working at something you enjoy.

If you treat everyone around you with respect and understanding — knowing that when you invest yourself in other lives, you will be greatly rewarded down the road.

If you have a place to come home to at the end of the day that feels like a sanctuary for your spirit and a garden for your soul.

If you can look back on decisions you've made with a confident heart, a clear conscience, and the understanding that for the most part you'd make the same choices all over again.

If you wake up every morning looking forward to whatever the day ahead might bring — knowing that difficulties are only temporary but the good things last forever.

If you have a dream that draws out the best in you — one that spurs your greatest efforts and influences you to continue improving your skills on a daily basis.

If you know how lucky you are to be in the world at this particular place and time... and to have so much to be grateful for...

If you are blessed with even a few of these — the greatest gifts in life — then you truly are richer than you think.

— Jon Peyton

Every Day Is a Gift...

Be glad of life
because it gives you the chance
to love
    and to work
        and to play
        and to look at the stars.

— Henry Van Dyke

...So Make the Most of Each One

If you sit down at set of sun
And count the acts that you have done,
And, counting, find
One self-denying deed, one word
That eased the heart of him who heard,
One glance most kind
That fell like sunshine where it went —
Then you may count that day well spent.

— George Eliot

Hold On to Hope

Hope is a beautiful answer to many difficult questions. Hope only asks that you believe. Hope only wants you to receive. Hope is "hanging in there" until help arrives. Whenever a day didn't go as planned, hope is there as a comforting guide to help you understand.

Hope is a quiet, personal place where you can always take shelter. Hope is the warm and welcomed knowledge that beautiful possibilities exist. Hope is all these special things, and in simply knowing this:

When hope is all you've got...
    you still have got a lot.

— Collin McCarty

Give Thanks Through Prayer

A single grateful thought
toward heaven
is the most complete prayer.
— Gotthold Lessing

If the only prayer you say in
your whole life is "Thank you,"
that would suffice.
— Johannes Meister Eckhart

Give thanks to God
   And humbly pray
To serve Him well
   This new-born day.

Give thanks to God
   For friends and flowers,
For sunny days
   And cooling showers.

Give thanks to God,
   Fill well your part;
Let love divine
   Possess your heart.

Give thanks to God,
   His bounty see;
Be still and know,
   And grateful be.

         — Grenville Kleiser

For flowers that bloom about our feet,
Father, we thank Thee.
For tender grass so fresh, so sweet,
Father, we thank Thee.
For the song of bird and hum of bee,
For all things fair we hear or see,
Father in heaven, we thank Thee.

For blue of stream and blue of sky,
Father, we thank Thee.
For pleasant shade of branches high,
Father, we thank Thee.
For fragrant air and cooling breeze,
For beauty of the blooming trees,
Father in heaven, we thank Thee.

For this new morning with its light,
Father, we thank Thee.
For rest and shelter of the night,
Father, we thank Thee.
For health and food, for love and friends,
For everything Thy goodness sends,
Father in heaven, we thank Thee.

— Ralph Waldo Emerson

A Thankful Heart Soothes Your Soul

There are few things which bless and soothe the lives of others more, or do them more good, than the giving of thanks. It makes men feel that they are some use in the world, and that is one of the finest impulses to a better life. It cheers many a wearied heart with pleasant hope and bids many a man who is sad in mood take courage.

— Stopford A. Brooke

Gratitude is one of the nicest feelings a heart can have. It's a feeling that comes along for a very special reason — and it's a lovely thought that never goes away once it enters in. Gratitude joins together with precious memories and grateful hopes. It lives on, not for just a moment or a day, but through all the days that lie ahead.

— Marin McKay

Be Thankful for All the Wonderful Things About You...

- ⊚ Your individuality

- ⊚ Your confidence

- ⊚ Your body (just as it is)

- ⊚ Your creativity

- ⊚ Your sense of humor

- Your talents

- Your beliefs

- Your voice

- Your strength

- All the imperfections that add up to a perfect you

Celebrate all you are
and how much you are loved.
Honor the person you are
and all you're becoming.
Be reminded of how many people
look up to you and admire
all the goodness in your heart.
Reach out and feel the happiness
others wish for you.
Do the things
that bring sunlight to your heart
and add a touch of magic to your dreams.

— Linda E. Knight

Feel really good about who you are
and about all the great things you do!
Appreciate your uniqueness.
Acknowledge your talents
    and abilities.
Realize what a beautiful soul
    you have.
Understand the wonder within.

— Sydney Nealson

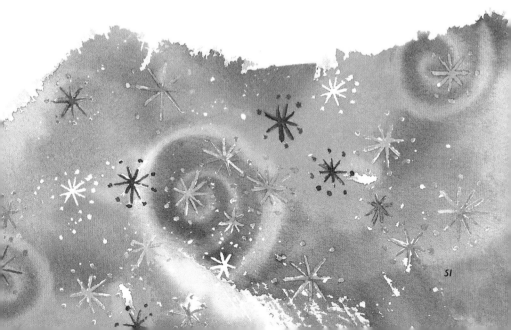

Don't Compare Yourself to Others

Sometimes you
think that you
need to be perfect
that you cannot
make mistakes
At these times
you put so much
pressure on yourself
Try to realize
that you are
a human being —
like everyone else
capable of
reaching great potential
but not capable of
being perfect

Just do your best
and realize that
this is enough
Don't compare yourself
to anyone
Be happy to be
the wonderful
unique, very special
person that you are
— Susan Polis Schutz

The Keys to a Grateful Heart

Always take time for...

Big smiles. Sunday mornings. Long walks.
Warm appreciation. Precious memories.
Things that bring a sense of joy to your
heart. Staying in touch... with the people
who will always mean so much.

Find a way to...

Be good to yourself (really good).
Build the bridges that will take you
everywhere you've ever wanted to
go. Write out your own definition of
success, and then do your absolute
best to make that story come true. Get
closer and closer to the summit of every
mountain you've ever wanted to climb.
Make the most... of your moment... of
this moment in time...

Make plans to...

Slow down the days. Find your perfect
pace. Be strong enough. Be gentle enough.
Reap the sweet rewards that will come from
all the good things you do and all the great
things you give. Keep things in perspective.

Remember to...

Invest wisely in the best riches of all.
Share invaluable words over warm cups
in quiet places. Treasure time spent in
heart-to-heart conversations. Laugh a
lot. Work it all out. Move ahead of every
worry. Move beyond any sorrows. Have
yourself a wealth of beautiful tomorrows.

— Douglas Pagels

We Are Made
for Gratitude

We are born with two eyes in front because we must not always look behind, but see what lies ahead beyond ourselves.

We are born to have two ears — one left, one right — so we can hear both sides, collect both the compliments and criticisms, to see which are right.

We are born with a brain concealed in a skull; no matter how poor we are, we are still rich, for no one can steal what our brain contains, packing in more jewels and rings than you can imagine.

We are born with two eyes, two ears, but one mouth, for the mouth is a sharp weapon — it can hurt, flirt, and kill. Remember our motto: talk less, listen, and see more.

We are born with only one heart; deep in our ribs, it reminds us to appreciate and give love from deep within.

— Author Unknown

Sometimes You Have to Search for the Good

Every night has its day. Every valley has its mountaintop. Every problem has a solution. Every down has its up. Every frown has a smile to it. You must be patient; wait and you will see.

Life is full of ups and downs — mountains and valleys, smiles and frowns. But friendship is there to be found. Love is there to be found. Bright moments are there to be found... and therein lies the beauty.

— Ashley Rice

The world was made
to be beautiful —
but sometimes we get caught up in
everyday actions
completely forgetting about this
completely forgetting that what
is truly important
are the simple, basic things in life —
honest, pure emotions
surrounded by the majestic beauty of nature

We need to concentrate on
the freeness and peacefulness of nature
and not on the driven material aspects of life
We need to smell the clear air
after the rainfall
and appreciate the good in things

We need to remember that
we are here for a short time
and that every day should count for
     something and
that every day we should be thankful
for all the natural beauty
The world is a wonderful place
and we are so lucky to be a part of it

— Susan Polis Schutz

Set Your Thoughts on the Good Things in Life

Think about some of the good things in life, like sunshine, holidays, feeling loved, special friendships, and laughter. Think about rainbows, butterflies, and beautiful sunsets and feel loved, cared about, and accepted. Remember that in life, although there is some bad stuff, good things really do happen too.

— Maria Mullins

There is always something
for which to be thankful.
— Charles Dickens

The mere sense of living is joy enough.
— Emily Dickinson

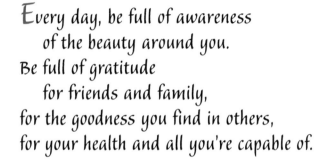

Every day, be full of awareness
of the beauty around you.
Be full of gratitude
for friends and family,
for the goodness you find in others,
for your health and all you're capable of.

Be full of acceptance
    of yourself and others —
without conditions or judging,
knowing that differences and changes
    make life interesting.
Appreciate the gifts of laughter
    and fun in your life,
and find contentment in knowing
    that you can always control
your ability to look on the bright side.

— Barbara Cage

See Setbacks as Chances to Grow

Life is forever changing. You can't always control what happens, but you can hang tough through it all. You can make the changes and decisions that are so necessary and will help you grow in spite of the disappointments, develop courage in spite of the adversities, be creative and come up with solutions, and always keep gratitude in your heart.

— Donna Levine-Small

Do not be bothered or discouraged by adversity. Instead, meet it as a challenge. Be empowered by the courage it takes you to overcome obstacles.

— Ashley Rice

The only real mistake we make is the one from which we learn nothing.

— John Wesley Powell

Be thankful that you don't already have
    everything you desire.
If you did, what would there be to look forward to?
Be thankful when you don't know something,
for it gives you the opportunity to learn.
Be thankful for the difficult times.
During those times, you grow.
Be thankful for your limitations,
because they give you opportunities for
    improvement.

Be thankful for each new challenge,
because it will build your strength and character.
Be thankful for your mistakes.
They will teach you valuable lessons.
Be thankful when you're tired and weary,
because it means you've made an effort.
It's easy to be thankful for the good things.
A life of rich fulfillment comes to those who
    are also thankful for the setbacks.
Gratitude can turn a negative into a positive.
Find a way to be thankful for your troubles,
and they can become your blessings.

— Author Unknown

Leave the Past Behind You

Finish every day and be done with it. You have done what you could. Some blunders and absurdities no doubt crept in; forget them as soon as you can. Tomorrow is a new day; begin it well and serenely and with too high a spirit to be cumbered with your old nonsense. This day is all that is good and fair. It is too dear, with its hopes and invitations, to waste a moment on yesterdays.

— Ralph Waldo Emerson

Travel the road that you have chosen,
and don't look back with regret.
— Jacqueline Schiff

Don't let old mistakes or
misfortunes hold you down: learn
from them, forgive yourself... or
others... and move on.
— Ashley Rice

Celebrate Life Today

There is a wonderful life waiting to be lived. Celebrate it today; life is too short to put off living until tomorrow.

Live it fully. Love its changes and choices. Let it surprise you. Let it show you new ways of doing old things. Let it help you explore and discover. Let it introduce you to people you have never known; to dreams you have never dreamed; to seeds you have never sown.

Let life take away some of your worries and caress your woes. Let it help you wonder and laugh and love. Let it show you how to rise with the sun and aim for the stars. Let it reveal how to reach out and become all that you are.

Let life challenge and encourage you. Let it stimulate and arouse you. Let it embrace and enfold you. Let it show you the majesty of a simple, peaceful morning. Let it show you the miracle of your complexity. Let it help you find your belief and discover your god. Let it amaze you with its possibilities.

Let life help you realize that
    it is what you make it and
        that it can be everything
            you want it to be.

— Collin McCarty

More Things to Be Thankful For...

- ◉ Shooting stars

- ◉ Three-day weekends

- ◉ Chocolate

- ◉ Smiles from strangers

- ◉ The courage to step out of your comfort zone

- ◉ Faith

- The inherent joy of children

- Laughter

- Happy memories

- Silence or noise (whichever you happen to have at the moment)

- The place you call home

Keep It Simple

Where are all the people
who enjoyed simple things
who used to go out in the sunlight
and sing songs as they gardened
stopping and talking with all the neighbors?
Where are all the people
who enjoyed life
who used to consider the home
the most important place to be
and who used to consider the family
the most important people to be with?
Times have changed most of these people
and urged them to seek the complicated
Yet it is only the very basic simple things in life
that can make people truly
happy

— Susan Polis Schutz

To find the universal elements enough; to find the air and the water exhilarating; to be refreshed by a morning walk or an evening saunter... to be thrilled by the stars at night; to be elated over a bird's nest or a wildflower in spring — these are some of the rewards of the simple life.

— John Burroughs

Smile Often

What sunshine is to flowers, smiles are to humanity. They are but trifles to be sure; but, scattered along life's pathway, the good they do is inconceivable.

— Joseph Addison

Life is made up of little things —
in which smiles and kindnesses are
what win and preserve the heart.

— Sir H. Davy

Try each day to make a smile grow...
and with each low, descending sun,
there will be at least two people who
will be glad, and one of them will be you.

— John Edwin Price

Put Your Feelings into Words

Gratitude is the hardest of all
emotions to express.
There is no word capable of
conveying all that one feels.
Until we reach a world
where thoughts can be
adequately expressed in words,
   "thank you"
      will have to do.

— A. P. Gouthey

Feeling gratitude and not expressing
it is like wrapping a present and not
giving it.

— William Arthur Ward

Sometimes it's hard to know what to say to convey your appreciation. But the truth of the matter is this: you don't need the perfect words. A simple thanks that comes from the heart... is always the sweetest response. You can speak it, write it, mail it, or share it many different ways (especially these days). If there's a thank-you that needs to be said, no matter how long it's been, it's important to say it... and incredibly nice for it to be heard.

The best gratitude... is expressed gratitude.

— Douglas Pagels

Practice the Art of Appreciation

If we knew how much the habit of being thankful might do for us, I am sure we would take time out every day to count up a few of our blessings. When the spirit of thankfulness takes its place in our consciousness, we radiate life from the very center of our being to the world about us.

— Author Unknown

You say grace before meals. All right. But I say grace before the concert and the opera, and grace before the play and pantomime, and grace before I open a book, and grace before sketching, painting, swimming, fencing, boxing, walking, playing, dancing, and grace before I dip the pen in the ink.

— G. K. Chesterton

Learn to See How Blessed You Are

Be grateful for the growing trees,
    the roses soon to bloom,
The tenderness of kindly hearts that
    shared your days of gloom;
Be grateful for the morning dew,
    the grass beneath your feet,
The soft caresses of your babes and
    all their laughter sweet.

Acquire the grateful habit, learn to see
    how blessed you are,
How much there is to gladden life,
    how little life to mar!
And what if rain shall fall today and
    you with grief are sad;
Be grateful that you can recall
    the joys that you have had.

— Edgar A. Guest

You Already Have All These Gifts Within You

Joy
  in your heart,
  your mind,
  your soul.
Happiness
  with yourself
  and with the world.
Harmony.
Courage
  to feel, to need,
  to reach out.
Freedom
  to let yourself
  be bound by love.

Wisdom
    to learn, to change,
    to let go.
Acceptance
    of the truth
    and beauty within yourself.
Growth.
Pleasure
    in all that you see
    and touch
    and do.
Peace
    with yourself
    and with the universe.

— Maureen Doan

Believe in Miracles

Every morning, wake with the awe
    of just being alive.
Each day, discover the magnificent,
    awesome beauty in the world.
Explore and embrace life in yourself
    and in everyone you see each day.
Reach within to find your own specialness.
Amaze yourself,
        and rouse those around you
            to the potential of each new day.

Don't be afraid to admit that you are
less than perfect;
    this is the essence of your humanity.
Let those who love you help you.
Trust enough to be able to take.
Look with hope to the horizon of today,
    for today is all we truly have.
Live this day well.
Let a little sunshine out as well as in.
Create your own rainbows.
Be open to all your possibilities;
    possibilities can be miracles.
Always believe in miracles!

— Vickie M. Worsham

Each day brings with it the miracle of a new beginning. Distractions abound, but whatever you do, don't miss the miracles.

— Douglas Pagels

The world will never starve for want of wonders; but only for want of wonder.

— G. K. Chesterton

Everything is miraculous. It is a miracle
that one does not melt in one's bath.

— Pablo Picasso

To me every hour of the light and dark
is a miracle. Every cubic inch of space is
a miracle.

— Walt Whitman

Any man who does not believe in miracles
is not a realist.

— David Ben Gurion

Take Pleasure in the Little Things

If you want to live more, you must master the art of appreciating the little, everyday blessings of life. This is not altogether a golden world, but there are countless gleams of gold to be discovered in it if we give our minds to them.

— Henry Alford Porter

Sing a song
Read a poem
Paint a picture
Dance to the music in your head
Rise up
and touch the stars —
today
— Susan Polis Schutz

Give Thanks for Good Friends and All the Times They've...

- Supported you

- Made you laugh

- Bought you a present

- Cheered you up

- Really listened

- Read your mind

- Appreciated you

- Been honest with you

- Forgiven you

- Hugged you

- Taken you out to dinner

- Celebrated with you

- Cried with you

- Encouraged you

- Loved you

Family Is One of Life's Greatest Gifts

The best feeling in this world
　　is family.
From it, we draw love,
　　friendship, moral support,
and the fulfillment of every
　　special need within our hearts.
In a family, we are connected to
　　an ever-present source
of sunny moments, smiles and laughter,
understanding and encouragement,
and hugs that help us grow
　　in confidence all along life's path.

Wherever we are,
whatever we're doing,
whenever we really need to feel
    especially loved, befriended,
    supported, and cared for
        in the greatest way,
we can turn to family
and find the very best
    always waiting for us.

— Barbara J. Hall

The Best Things in Life Are Free

The best things in life are nearest: breath in your nostrils, light in your eyes, flowers at your feet, duties at your hand, the path of right just before you. Then do not grasp at the stars, but do life's plain, common work as it comes, certain that daily duties and daily bread are the sweetest things in life.

— Robert Louis Stevenson

The priceless gifts we give each other
are not the ones wrapped
in fancy paper,
but the gifts we give when
we give of ourselves.
It is the love that we share.
It is the comfort we lend in times of need.
It is the moments we spend together
helping each other follow our dreams.
The most priceless gifts we can give
are the understanding and caring
that come from the heart.
And each and every one of us
has these gifts to offer...
through the gift of ourselves.

— Ben Daniels

Be Generous with All You've Been Given

The generous heart is the happy heart. If you have beautiful thoughts, why should you hoard them? If you have wonderful gifts, why should you hide them? If you have a warm, loving hand, why should you close it against your breast instead of opening it in cordial greeting to your brother man? One little act of generosity is a small thing, yet you cannot perform the most trivial task which will be a blessing to someone else without being benefited by it yourself. Someone has said, "Charity is never lost; it may meet with ingratitude, or be of no service to those on whom it was bestowed, yet it ever does a work of beauty and grace upon the heart of the giver."

— Ida Scott Taylor

Two kinds of gratitude: the sudden kind
we feel for what we take, the larger kind
we feel for what we give.

— Edwin Arlington Robinson

Pay It Forward

You will find, as you look back on your life, that the moments that stand out are the moments when you have done things for others.

— Henry Drummond

After the verb "To Love," "To Help" is the most beautiful verb in the world.

— Bertha von Suttner

Always help light the way for others.
Think of it not as your work
or even your purpose,
but as your destiny.

— Jane Almarie Lewis

We need to feel more
to understand others
We need to love more
to be loved back
We need to cry more
to cleanse ourselves
We need to laugh more
to enjoy ourselves

We need to establish the values
   of honesty and fairness
when interacting with people
We need to establish
   a strong ethical basis
as a way of life

We need to see more
other than our own little fantasies
We need to hear more
and listen to the needs of others

We need to give more
and take less
We need to share more
and own less
We need to realize
    the importance of the family
as a backbone to stability
We need to look more
and realize that we are not
    so different from one another

We need to create a world where
we can all peacefully live
the life we choose
We need to create a world where
we can trust each other

— Susan Polis Schutz

On the Receiving End of Generosity

Be thankful for the smallest blessing, and you will deserve to receive greater. Value the least gifts no less than the greatest, and simple graces as especial favors. If you remember the dignity of the Giver, no gift will seem small or mean.

— Thomas à Kempis

To receive honestly is the best thanks for a good thing.

— George Macdonald

There is as much greatness of mind in acknowledging a good turn, as in doing it.

— Seneca

If You Look for Something to Be Grateful for, You Will Find It

Look for something to be thankful and glad over each day, and you will find it. Consider each disappointment and trouble as so much experience and as a temporary lesson set for you to learn...

Go forth with calmness and new strength to face the world...

No one can harm you if you do not harm yourself. Fill your soul and mind so full of love and sympathy and joy that nothing lesser can find accommodation.

— Ella Wheeler Wilcox

Just to look at the sun going down behind green hills; just to watch rain falling on a quiet lake; just to see spinning tops of sand, created by winds whirling over a desert; just to be able to imagine oneself upon a ship, docking at a pier in a strange and distant port; just to be able to touch the hand of another and feel oneself become a part of that other; just to breathe the evening air and hear the voices of children, raised in laughter; O! just to feel one is a part of all the scheme of things entire — such are the blessings humans have.

— G. Allison Phelps

Even More Things to Be Thankful For...

- ◉ Clothes that fit just right

- ◉ Good food

- ◉ A comfortable chair

- ◉ The chance to enjoy your favorite TV show

- ◉ A clean house

- ◉ Fresh air

- ◉ Inventions and technology that make your life easier (and more enjoyable too)

◉ Freedom

◉ New beginnings

◉ An open mind and an open heart

◉ Answered prayers

◉ The endless possibilities for joy, love, fun, and peace that each moment holds

Take These Blessings with You Everywhere You Go

Love — to shine like blue skies above you wherever you go, so you always know you're in the hearts of so many people.

Light — to see the end of the tunnel when you're struggling with troubles, so you always know you have the inner power to survive and triumph.

Laughter — to keep you healthy in mind and body; to give you the ability to tell great jokes, act silly, and exercise your giggle; to remind you that life is too short to be taken so seriously.

A lifeline — to anchor you, support you, and keep you going forward in a positive way when you're faced with a crisis, so you always know you are a survivor.

Lots of good luck — to help you fulfill all your wishes, so you always know your possibilities are unlimited — and success is your destiny.

— Jacqueline Schiff

Gratitude Opens Doors

Always see the goodness in this world,
do your part in helping those
     less fortunate,
walk hand in hand with those
     of less talent,
follow those of more knowledge,
and be an equal with those
     who are different.
Find your special purpose
     in this world so full of choices,
and help lead those who stray.
Become your own individual —
set yourself apart from those who
     are the same.

Have the self-confidence to say no
    when it is necessary
and the strength to stand alone.
Give yourself the approval to love and
    respect everything that you are
    and will become.
Reap the fruits of your talents,
walk with pride down the road of life,
be humble in your successes,
and share in the praises and joy of others.
Most of all, be grateful.
For when you are grateful,
    you have the key that will open all
    of the world's doors to you.

— Jackie Olson

Choose to Be Grateful Every Day

Life can make choices for us.
Sometimes these choices
    seem unhappy or unfair,
but in the end, we control
our own destiny because we can decide
    how people and events affect us.

So much of our happiness lies within
the choices we make.
We can accept that life
isn't the way we want it to be,
or we can change it so that it will be...

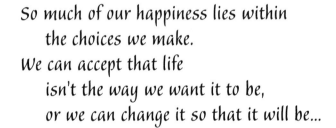

We can walk through the shadows,
  or we can choose to smile
  and seek out the sunlight.
We can create grand dreams
  that never leave the ground,
  or we can be builders of dreams that come true.
We can look at only the negative aspects of ourselves,
  or we can lift ourselves up
  by being our own best friend.

We can live in the past
   or dream about the future,
   or we can live for today.
We can give up when the road becomes difficult,
   or we can keep on going
   until the view is much better.
The choices in life are endless,
   and so is the potential for gratitude.

— Nancye Sims

May You Always Have Reasons to Be Thankful

May your life be filled with the joy of friends and family, and may each day bring you the pleasures and deep rewards of love and friendship ◎ May your heart be at peace, and in unsteady and uncertain times, may you always have something to hold on to as a source of comfort and peace in your thoughts, your beliefs, and your life ◎ May your efforts be always rewarded, and may you experience the joy of achievement and always have the excitement of meaningful challenges ◎

May you always find the things that most matter to you ◎ May your responsibilities still leave you with the time and freedom for the people and activities that provide your deepest satisfaction ◎ May the end of every journey provide a chance for reflection and appreciation for everyone who helped you and for everything you gained along the way ◎ May you always have reasons for giving thanks ◎

— Garry LaFollette

ACKNOWLEDGMENTS

We gratefully acknowledge the permission granted by the following authors and authors' representatives to reprint poems or excerpts from their publications.

Susan Polis Schutz for "Where are all the people who...," "Sometimes you think that you...," "We don't often take the time...," "The world was made to be beautiful...," and "Sing a song...." Copyright © 1982, 1986, 1990, 1993, 2001 by Stephen Schutz and Susan Polis Schutz. And for "We need to feel more...." Copyright © 1972 by Continental Publications. Renewed © 2000 by Stephen Schutz and Susan Polis Schutz. All rights reserved.

PrimaDonna Entertainment Corp. for "Live Every Day with a Thankful Heart" by Donna Fargo. Copyright © 2010 by PrimaDonna Entertainment Corp. All rights reserved.

Barbara Cage for "Ten Ways to Cultivate Gratitude." Copyright © 2014 by Barbara Cage. All rights reserved.

Barbara J. Hall for "Welcome Each Blessing." Copyright © 2014 by Barbara J. Hall. All rights reserved.

A careful effort has been made to trace the ownership of selections used in this anthology in order to obtain permission to reprint copyrighted material and give proper credit to the copyright owners. If any error or omission has occurred, it is completely inadvertent, and we would like to make corrections in future editions provided that written notification is made to the publisher:

BLUE MOUNTAIN ARTS, INC., P.O. Box 4549, Boulder, Colorado 80306.